Selected Duets

for CORNET or TRUMPET

by H. VOXMAN

T0071584

Published In Two Volumes:

● VOLUME I (Easy - Medium)   VOLUME II (Advanced)

RUBANK ®

HAL•LEONARD ®
CORPORATION

7777 W. BLUEMOUND RD. P.O. BOX 13819 MILWAUKEE, WI 53213

Nine Duets
Selected from the Works of Korda

KORDA

PETITE WALTZ

KORDA

Allegretto (fast three)

CANON

KORDA

Moderato

MARCH IN G

KORDA

March time

POLONAISE

KORDA

Allegro moderato

HUNTING SCENE

KORDA

MINUET

KORDA

RUSTIC MARCH

KORDA

EVENING STORY

KORDA

Twenty-Two Duets
Selected from the Works of
Guericke, Haag, Metzger, and others

OLD GERMAN SONG

RATHGEBER

CHRISTMAS SONG

Old Dutch

THERE RODE THREE HORSEMEN

German

Allegretto

3

HUNTING SONG

German

Lively

4

MENUET

18th Century

ADAGIO

18th Century

GIGUE

18th Century

CHORUS FROM "PRECIOSA"

von WEBER

MOZART

Larghetto (♩ = 116)

9

mp legato

MENUET
(The Cuckoo)

18th Century

Allegretto (In three)

10

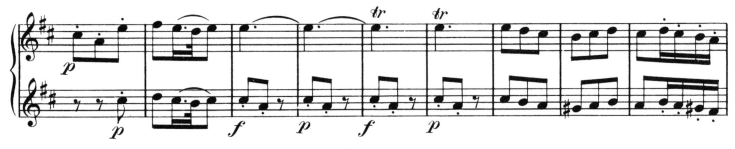

Allegro non troppo

METZGER

METZGER

Merrily

METZGER

Allegretto

GUERICKE

14

Lustily

GUERICKE

15

poco allargando

PROCESSIONAL

HAAG

HAAG

TIME STUDY

HAAG

JUMPING DANCE

HAAG

MENUET

HAAG

TRIO

MUSETTE

18th Century

GIGA

SNOW

Five Duets
Selected from the Works of Clodomir

CLODOMIR

CLODOMIR

Moderato

Allegretto (♩=132)

CLODOMIR

3

CLODOMIR

Eleven Studies in Canon Form
Selected from the Works of Bagantz

BAGANTZ

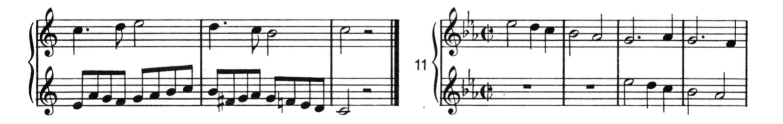

Twelve Duets

Selected from the Works of
Boismortier, Gatti, St. Jacome, and others

RONDINETTO

St. JACOME

St. JACOME

2

MINUETTO

Allegretto

STAMITZ

3

TRIO

RONDO

La BARRE

TAMBURIN

CHÉDEVILLE

Andantino

6

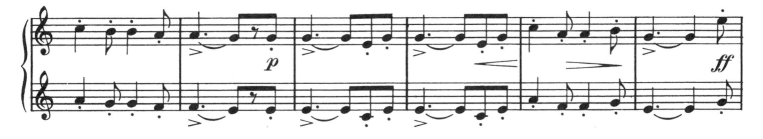

BOISMORTIER

GIGUE

BOISMORTIER

ALLEMANDE

BOISMORTIER

Allegro moderato

BAUSTETTER

Six Duets

Selected from the Works of Forestier

FORESTIER

48

Andante sostenuto
Religioso

Poco più vivo

Allegretto

FORESTIER

Allegretto

2

Adagio

FORESTIER

Allegro moderato

3

mf sempre staccato

Andante sostenuto

Allegretto

Adagio

Allegretto

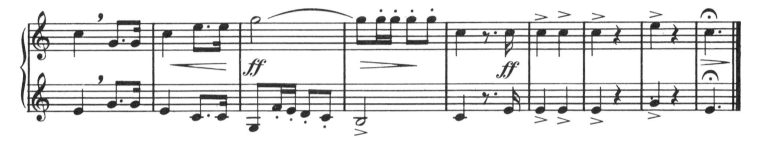

FORESTIER

58

Adagio

Allegretto

FORESTIER

Allegro

6

Lento

Tempo di Valse

D.S. al Fine

Six Duos
Selected from the Works of Rossari

ROSSARI

Andante religioso assai largo

1

Allegro non tanto

2

Allegretto festoso

3

p brillante

staccato assai

Moderato

Moderato

5

Moderato (Allegro maestoso)

6